Fre the Frog

Written by Joyce Dunbar

Illustrated By
Dennis Hockerman

Freddie the Frog
is fond of his pond.

So fond of his pond
that he sits there each day,
thinking of pond games
and pond tricks to play.

"Today is a hop day,"
he says on day one.
"On hop days, I like to have
hip-hoppy fun.

I go hop, I go plop,
I go flip flappy flop!
Oh, hop days are fun
for a frog on the hop."

"Today is a slip day,"
he says on day two.
"I go slip, I go slop,
and I slide about, too.

Oh, slip sloppy slap!
Oh, slop slappy slip!
Slip days slide by
for a frog feeling flip!"

"Today is a splish day,"
he says on day three.
"I go splish. I go splosh.
Oh, come splashing with me!

Oh, splish splashy splosh!
Oh, splosh splashy splish!
For what more in the world
could a happy frog wish?"

"Today is a jump day,"
he says on day four.
"I can jump, I can flump.
Oh, what frog can do more?

Oh, the joy of a jump over bump! Over hump! Up! Up! And then down, with a slip-slappy thump."

On day five, still alive,
he simply gets wet.
On day six, full of tricks,
he is not tired yet.

But now it's day seven.
Day seven is best,
for that is when Freddie
takes time for a rest.

He paddles in puddles
and looks up at the sky
and down at the beetles
and bugs floating by.

With a flick of his tongue
and a chop-smacking munch,
Freddie the Frog
fills his belly with lunch.

Then he blinks while he sinks
in the mud by his pond
and thinks, sits and thinks,
just how fond, oh how fond,
he is of his flip-floppy
plip-ploppy pond.